This is a guide to making Profit with your book from Idea to Publishing.

Table of Contents

1. Introduction
2. Embracing the Authorpreneur Mindset
3. Writing with Purpose
4. Crafting Your Book Summary
5. The Editing Process
6. Building Your Brand
7. Effective Marketing Strategies
8. Leveraging Social Media
9. Exploring Diverse Revenue Streams
10. Creating a Course from Your Book
11. Engaging with Your Audience
12. Launching Your Book
13. Measuring Success
14. Overcoming Challenges
15. Continuous Learning and Improvement
16. Building Your Authorpreneur Empire
17. Summary and Conclusion

1. Introduction

Welcome to "Guide to Authorpreneurship," where I'll share my journey and insights to help you turn your writing into a profitable venture. Writing a book is just the beginning; being an authorpreneur involves embracing both creativity and business acumen.

---

2. Embracing the Authorpreneur Mindset

My Experience

When I started, I was solely focused on writing. Realizing the need to think like a businessperson transformed my career. Understanding the publishing industry, setting clear goals, and being prepared to invest in myself were crucial steps.

Tips

- **Develop a Business Plan**: Outline your goals, target audience, and marketing strategy.
- **Stay Informed**: Keep up with industry trends and changes.
- **Invest in Learning**: Attend workshops, webinars, and read books on marketing and entrepreneurship.

Questions to Ask

- What are my long-term career goals?
- How can I balance creativity and business?
- What resources are available to help me learn more about the industry?

---

3. Writing with Purpose

My Experience

Early in my career, I wrote without a clear direction. Defining my genre and audience helped me write with more focus and purpose.

Tips

- **Identify Your Genre**: Decide whether you want to write fiction, nonfiction, or a hybrid.
- **Know Your Audience**: Research who your readers are and what they want.
- **Plan Your Story**: Outline your plot or main ideas before you start writing.

Questions to Ask

- Who is my ideal reader?
- What message or story do I want to convey?
- How can I make my writing stand out in my chosen genre?

4. Crafting Your Book Summary

My Experience

Writing a compelling book summary was one of my first marketing tasks. It was challenging but crucial for capturing readers' attention.

Tips

- **Keep it Short**: Aim for 100-175 words.
- **Highlight the Hook**: What makes your book unique?
- **Focus on Benefits**: What will readers gain from your book?

Questions to Ask

- What is the central theme of my book?
- How can I summarize my book in a way that intrigues potential readers?
- What specific benefits does my book offer?

---

5. The Editing Process

My Experience

Editing is where the real work begins. I learned the importance of self-editing, beta-readers, and professional editors through trial and error.

Tips

- **Self-Edit First**: Read through your manuscript and make initial changes.
- **Use Beta-Readers**: Get feedback from people who fit your target demographic.
- **Hire a Professional Editor**: Consider both developmental and copy editors.

Questions to Ask

- Have I thoroughly self-edited my manuscript?
- Who can provide honest and constructive feedback?
- What kind of professional editing does my book need?

---

6. Building Your Brand

My Experience

Creating a personal brand was essential for establishing myself as a credible author. It involved consistent messaging across all platforms.

Tips

- **Define Your Brand**: What do you want to be known for?
- **Create a Website**: Your online hub for all information about you and your books.
- **Be Consistent**: Maintain a consistent voice and message across all platforms.

Questions to Ask

- What are my core values as an author?
- How can I create a strong online presence?
- What can I do to make my brand stand out?

---

7. Effective Marketing Strategies

My Experience

Marketing was daunting at first, but finding the right strategies was key to my success. Experimenting with different tactics helped me discover what worked best.

Tips

- **Use Email Marketing**: Build a mailing list and keep your readers informed.
- **Leverage Book Reviews**: Reach out to book bloggers and reviewers.
- **Run Promotions**: Use discounts and giveaways to attract new readers.

Questions to Ask

- What marketing channels are most effective for my audience?
- How can I build and maintain an email list?
- What promotional tactics can I use to boost book sales?

---

8. Leveraging Social Media

My Experience

Social media allowed me to connect directly with my readers. It became a powerful tool for engagement and promotion.

Tips

- **Choose the Right Platforms**: Focus on where your audience spends their time.
- **Engage Regularly**: Post consistently and interact with your followers.
- **Share Valuable Content**: Provide insights, updates, and behind-the-scenes looks.

Questions to Ask

- Which social media platforms are best for my target audience?
- How can I create engaging content?
- What strategies can I use to grow my social media following?

---

9. Exploring Diverse Revenue Streams

My Experience

Relying solely on book sales was limiting. Diversifying my income streams helped stabilize my earnings.

Tips

- **Offer Online Courses**: Share your expertise through webinars or courses.
- **Host Workshops**: Engage with readers and aspiring writers in person.
- **Create Merchandise**: Sell branded products related to your book.

Questions to Ask

- What additional products or services can I offer?
- How can I leverage my expertise to create new revenue streams?
- What partnerships can I form to expand my reach?

---

10. Creating a Course from Your Book

My Experience

Transforming my book into a course was a game-changer. It allowed me to reach a wider audience and generate additional income.

Tips

- **Identify Key Topics**: Break down your book into core lessons or modules.
- **Develop Course Material**: Create videos, workbooks, and quizzes to enhance learning.
- **Market Your Course**: Use your existing audience and social media to promote the course.

Example

When I turned my book on creative writing into an online course, I started by identifying the main concepts and developed comprehensive modules for each. I created engaging video content, downloadable resources, and interactive quizzes to ensure a rich learning experience.

Questions to Ask

- What are the main topics or lessons from my book that can be taught in a course?
- What format will best deliver the course content (e.g., video, written, interactive)?
- How can I effectively market my course to reach potential students?

11. Engaging with Your Audience

My Experience

Building a loyal reader base was vital. Engaging with my audience through various channels helped me establish lasting relationships.

Tips

- **Respond to Feedback**: Show appreciation for your readers' input.

- **Host Q&A Sessions**: Use social media or live events to interact with your audience.
- **Create a Community**: Start a reader group or book club.

Questions to Ask

- How can I encourage reader interaction?
- What platforms can I use to engage with my audience?
- How can I create a supportive community around my books?

---

12. Launching Your Book

My Experience

A successful book launch requires careful planning and execution. Coordinating with various stakeholders ensured a smooth launch process.

Tips

- **Set a Launch Date**: Plan well in advance.
- **Create a Launch Plan**: Outline steps and assign deadlines.
- **Collaborate with Influencers**: Partner with bloggers, authors, and media outlets.

Questions to Ask

- What is the best time to launch my book?
- Who can help me promote my book launch?
- What activities will generate the most buzz for my launch?

---

13. Measuring Success

My Experience

Tracking my progress was crucial for understanding what worked and what didn't. Metrics and feedback guided my future strategies.

Tips

- **Set Clear Goals**: Define what success looks like for you.
- **Use Analytics**: Track sales, website traffic, and social media engagement.
- **Gather Feedback**: Regularly ask for reader reviews and testimonials.

Questions to Ask

- What key performance indicators (KPIs) should I track?
- How can I use analytics to improve my marketing efforts?
- What feedback do I need to collect to gauge success?

14. Overcoming Challenges

My Experience

Facing and overcoming obstacles was part of my journey. Resilience and adaptability were key to navigating setbacks.

Tips

- **Stay Positive**: Maintain a positive outlook even during tough times.
- **Seek Support**: Connect with fellow authors and writing communities.
- **Adapt and Learn**: Be willing to adjust your strategies based on feedback and results.

Questions to Ask

- What are my biggest challenges as an authorpreneur?
- How can I stay motivated during difficult times?
- What resources are available to help me overcome obstacles?

---

15. Continuous Learning and Improvement

My Experience

The publishing industry is always evolving. Continuous learning helped me stay ahead and improve my craft.

Tips

- **Read Widely**: Keep up with industry news and trends.
- **Attend Conferences**: Network and learn from experts.
- **Invest in Professional Development**: Take courses and seek mentorship.

Questions to Ask

- What new skills do I need to develop?
- How can I stay updated with industry changes?
- Who can mentor me on my authorpreneur journey?

16. Building Your Authorpreneur Empire

Overview

Transforming from an author to an authorpreneur involves leveraging a published book to expand your business through various channels including merchandise, podcasts, blogs, digital products, courses, and public speaking.

Key Strategies

- **Creating a Blog**: Platforms, design, and content strategy. Writing compelling posts that attract and retain readers.
- **Starting a Podcast**: Choosing your podcast niche. Technical setup: Equipment, software, and hosting. Content planning and guest interviews.
- **Creating and Selling Digital Products**: Types of digital products: Workbooks, templates, webinars. Designing and pricing your products. Marketing and sales strategies.
- **Developing Online Courses**: Course creation: From idea to curriculum. Platforms for hosting and selling courses. Engaging students and maximizing enrollment.
- **Creating Merchandise**: Types of merchandise that complement your book. Designing and sourcing: From idea to production. Setting up an online store.

- **Building a Strong Personal Brand**: Defining your brand identity and message. Consistent branding across all platforms and products.
- **Becoming a Public Speaker**: Identifying speaking opportunities. Crafting your keynote and other presentations. Engaging your audience and building your speaking career.
- **Networking and Collaboration**: Building relationships within the industry. Collaborating with other authors and entrepreneurs. Utilizing social media for networking.

Personal Viewpoint and Encouragement from Edna White

When I first started my journey as an author, I had no idea what lay ahead. My story, my truth, had been buried deep inside me for years, hidden in shame, pain, and fear. It wasn't until I was in my 40s that I found the courage to write my first book, *Stuff! The Things No One Told Us About Life After Childhood Sexual Abuse.* That was a monumental moment for me, not just as an author but as a person learning to heal and share my story. For years, I kept my pain to myself. It wasn't something I wanted to admit to the world, and certainly not something I wanted to bring into the light of my family's knowledge.

For nearly a decade, I kept that manuscript tucked away, afraid of the consequences. I was afraid of what people would think, afraid of the judgment, and afraid of the backlash from my family when I revealed my truth about my perpetrator. Writing that book was terrifying. I remember feeling like the words would expose too much, take too much from me, and shatter everything I had worked so hard to keep intact. But in my heart, I knew I had to do it. I had to share my truth. I had to set myself free.

But it wasn't easy. The first time I submitted my manuscript, I faced rejection after rejection. Thirty rejections. Thirty "no's." I even submitted to Jimmy Swaggart Publishing, and they turned me down too.

That was hard. But instead of letting those rejections define me, I chose to let them fuel my determination. I kept going. I kept writing, revising, and submitting. With every "no," I learned something new. Each rejection taught me more about the industry, about writing, and most importantly, about myself. I began to realize that the journey wasn't about being perfect; it was about being persistent.

I won't lie—it was tough. There were times when I doubted myself, when I wondered if I was just wasting my time. But deep down, I knew I had a message that needed to be heard. I knew that someone out there was waiting to hear my story, to find comfort in my words, and to know that they were not alone in their pain. That kept me going.

Eventually, my persistence paid off. I didn't just write *Stuff!*; I wrote *Stuff!* from the heart. I didn't worry about perfection. I didn't worry about what others might think. I simply wrote what I felt. And that, I believe, was the key to everything. When I stopped focusing on making my words fit someone else's mold, I started writing the stories that were meant to be told.

Now, here I am, on my 32nd project. That's right—32 books later, and I've built a thriving author business. I'm not just an author anymore. I'm an authorpreneur, and I've learned that writing is just one part of the equation. Being an authorpreneur is about combining creativity with business strategy. It's about turning your passion for writing into a sustainable business, one that not only fulfills you creatively but also supports you financially.

It's a rewarding journey, but it's not without its challenges. There will always be obstacles along the way. You will face doubts, rejections, and setbacks. But I am here to tell you, from my own experience, that those challenges are not roadblocks—they are stepping stones. Every "no" is one step closer to a "yes." Every failure is an opportunity to learn, to grow, and to refine your craft.

When I first started this journey, I had no idea where it would take me. But with every project, every book, I learned something new. I kept adapting, kept evolving, and most importantly, I kept writing. And with each new project, I built a business. A business that sustains me and allows me to do what I love every single day.

So, to all the aspiring authors out there, I encourage you: don't give up. You will hear plenty of "no's" along the way, but don't let them stop you. Let them drive you to work harder, to push further, and to keep going. Remember, it's not about perfection. It's about persistence. Write what you feel. Don't worry about making mistakes—those mistakes are part of the process. The most important thing is to keep moving forward.

Being an authorpreneur is about more than just writing books. It's about turning your passion into a profitable business. It's about combining your creativity with a solid business strategy, and it's about continuously learning and adapting. The key to success is perseverance. Stay committed to your goals, embrace every challenge as an opportunity to grow, and never, ever give up.

I started with a dream of sharing my story with the world. Through perseverance, learning, and growing, I've built a business that supports me and allows me to do what I love. You can do it too. Believe in yourself, stay committed, and never be afraid to seek help or support. Your journey as an authorpreneur begins now, and I have no doubt you will succeed.

With best wishes on your journey,

Edna White

Bonus: Creative Marketing Ideas to Boost Your Book Sales

Marketing your book is just as important as writing it. Without effective promotion, even the best books can remain unnoticed. In this bonus section, I'll share some out-of-the-box ideas that will help you market your book and get it into the hands of the readers who need it most. Remember, each book is a unique project, and your marketing strategy should always align with the business plan and core message of your book. Here are some creative strategies to consider:

1. Host Virtual Book Launch Parties

In today's digital world, virtual events are a fantastic way to engage readers from all over the world. Host a virtual book launch party on platforms like Zoom, Facebook Live, or YouTube. You can offer exclusive sneak peeks, talk about the inspiration behind your book, answer questions from readers, and even give away signed copies or special bonuses. The key is to make it interactive and fun!

2. Create an Engaging Book Trailer

Think of a book trailer like a movie trailer but for your book. A short, compelling video can capture the essence of your book in just a few seconds, leaving viewers intrigued and wanting more. Post your trailer on social media, your website, and even YouTube to increase visibility. Use professional services or simple DIY tools to create something engaging that can be easily shared.

3. Leverage Your Expertise – Host Webinars or Workshops

If your book is non-fiction or provides valuable insights, you can create webinars or online workshops based on the content of your book. This positions you as an expert and encourages people to purchase your book to dive deeper into the subject matter. For example, if your book is about personal development or business strategy, offer free or low-cost webinars that promote the principles in your book while leading viewers to buy a copy for more detailed advice.

4. Partner with Influencers and Bloggers

Collaborating with influencers or bloggers in your niche can help spread the word about your book to a wider audience. Look for individuals who align with the themes of your book and are interested in promoting content to their followers. Offer them a free copy of your book in exchange for an honest review or a social media shout-out. When an influencer shares your book with their audience, it can create significant buzz and drive sales.

5. Utilize Instagram Reels and TikTok

Short-form video content is incredibly popular, and platforms like Instagram and TikTok provide a great opportunity to create fun, engaging videos that can go viral. Use these platforms to share quick insights, tips, behind-the-scenes content, or even humorous takes on the book's themes. Hashtags like #BookTok and #Bookstagram can help your posts gain traction among readers who are passionate about discovering new books.

6. Create a Book Companion Website or Blog

A website dedicated to your book can be a great way to engage with readers. Include book excerpts, a detailed author bio, behind-the-scenes content, a blog about topics related to your book, and even a community forum for readers to discuss your work. A blog can also be a platform for SEO, helping your book show up when people search for topics related to your genre or subject matter. Make sure to have a clear call-to-action that drives readers to purchase your book.

7. Run a Social Media Contest or Giveaway

Giveaways are a great way to create buzz around your book. Offer free signed copies, merchandise, or exclusive content in exchange for social media engagement. For example, you could ask participants to follow your account, share your post, and tag friends who might be interested in your book. This not only builds excitement around your book but also encourages word-of-mouth marketing.

8. Offer a Limited-Time Discount or Bundle Deals

Everyone loves a good deal! Offer a limited-time discount or bundle your book with other products, such as exclusive downloadable content, workbooks, or merchandise related to the themes of your book. Bundle deals or discounts can encourage people to buy your book and share it with friends, ultimately helping you expand your reader base.

9. Plan Monthly Book Signings and Author Appearances

Book signings are a timeless way to connect with readers face-to-face. Organize monthly book signings, either in local bookstores, libraries, or community centers. If physical signings aren't possible, host virtual signings through Zoom or Facebook Live. Creating a personal connection with your readers builds loyalty and encourages repeat sales. You can also expand your reach by participating in author panels, podcasts, or speaking engagements. This increases your visibility and establishes you as a trusted figure in your niche.

10. Create an Email Newsletter for Fans

Building an email list is a great way to create a loyal fan base. Offer a free downloadable resource, such as a chapter excerpt, in exchange for readers signing up for your newsletter. Use the newsletter to share exclusive content, sneak peeks of upcoming books, or special promotions. Email marketing is a highly effective tool for keeping your readers engaged and reminding them to purchase your latest book.

11. Create Merchandise Based on Your Book

T-shirts, mugs, tote bags, and posters featuring quotes or themes from your book are fun ways to spread awareness and create an additional revenue stream. Use platforms like Etsy or Redbubble to sell merchandise related to your book. This not only markets your book but also helps you build a brand around your author persona.

12. Collaborate with Other Authors

Form partnerships with other authors in your genre to cross-promote your books. You can do joint book launches, collaborative giveaways, or even write guest posts for each other's blogs. By tapping into each other's audiences, you can expand your reach and increase book sales.

13. Engage with Book Clubs

Reach out to book clubs, both local and online, and offer them a special deal to read your book. Offer to join them for a virtual discussion or answer questions about the book. Book clubs are always looking for new material, and your book could be the next one they want to dive into. This personal connection can generate word-of-mouth recommendations and repeat customers.

The Key to Success

When marketing your book, remember that consistency is key. Align each marketing strategy with your book's message and audience, and keep evolving your approach as you learn what works best for your unique situation. Every marketing effort, big or small, contributes to your book's success. Whether you're hosting a book signing or sharing content on social media, each touchpoint with your audience helps build your author brand and grow your readership.

With persistence, creativity, and the right strategies, you can turn your book into a thriving business. Never stop learning, and always look for new and innovative ways to engage with your readers. You have the power to create a lasting impact and build a career you love as an authorpreneur.

www.ingramcontent.com/pod-product-compliance
Lightning Source LLC
Chambersburg PA
CBHW072057230526
45479CB00010B/1121